understanding
mental health

FETAL ALCOHOL SPECTRUM DISORDER

ELLEN RODGER AND ROSIE GOWSELL

Crabtree Publishing Company
www.crabtreebooks.com

understanding mental health

Developed and produced by Plan B Book Packagers
www.planbbookpackagers.com
Authors: Ellen Rodger and Rosie Gowsell
Editorial director: Ellen Rodger
Art director: Rosie Gowsell-Pattison
Project coordinator: Kathy Middleton
Editor: Molly Aloian
Proofreader: Wendy Scavuzzo
**Production coordinator and prepress
    technician:** Tammy McGarr
Print coordinator: Margaret Amy Salter

Photographs:
Cover, Title page: Piotr Marcinski/Shutterstock.com;
p. 4: violetblue/Shutterstock.com; p. 5: ptashka/
Shutterstock.com; p. 6: Linda Bucklin/ Shutterstock.com;
p. 7: Monkey Business Images/ Shutterstock.com;
p. 8: cristovao/Shutterstock.com; p. 10: mast3r/
Shutterstock.com; p. 12: cowboy54/ Shutterstock.com;
p. 13: Petrenko Andriy/ Shutterstock.com; p. 14: vita
khorzhevska/ Shutterstock.com; p. 15: Krivosheev Vitaly/
Shutterstock.com; p. 16-17: BortN66/Shutterstock.com;
p. 18: Masson/Shutterstock.com; p. 19: Gina Callaway/
Shutterstock.com; p. 20: Dmitry Naumov/
Shutterstock.com; p. 21: Sergey Nivens/ Shutterstock.com;
p. 22: (left) Bevan Goldswain/ Shutterstock.com; p. 22:
(bottom) Viktor Gladkov/ Shutterstock.com; p. 23:
iQoncept/Shutterstock.com; p. 24: Martin Allinger/
Shutterstock.com; p. 25: Iakov Filimonov/
Shutterstock.com; p. 26: Suzanne Tucker/
Shutterstock.com; p. 28: Aleshyn_Andrei/
Shutterstock.com; p. 30: Monkey Business Images/
Shutterstock.com; p. 31: MR.LIGHTMAN/
Shutterstock.com; p. 32: Red-Blue Photo/ Shutterstock.com;
p. 33: Szasz-Fabian Ilka Erika/ Shutterstock.com; p. 34:
Lightspring/Shutterstock.com; p. 35: Dusaleev
Viatcheslav/Shutterstock.com; p. 36: Ryan Jorgensen -
Jorgo/Shutterstock.com; p. 37: Elena Elisseeva/
Shutterstock.com; p. 38: art4all/ Shutterstock.com; p. 40:
Joy Prescott/Shutterstock.com; p. 41: Joy Prescott/
Shutterstock.com; p. 42: Max Topchii/Shutterstock.com;
p. 43: Maxx-Studio/Shutterstock.com; p. 44: (right) iofoto/
Shutterstock.com; p. 44: (bottom) Jeff Lueders/
Shutterstock.com; p. 45: iodrakon/Shutterstock.com

Library and Archives Canada Cataloguing in Publication

Rodger, Ellen, author
    Fetal alcohol spectrum disorder / Ellen Rodger,
Rosie Gowsell.

(Understanding mental health)
Includes index.
Issued in print and electronic formats.
ISBN 978-0-7787-0083-8 (bound).--ISBN 978-0-7787-0089-0 (pbk.).--
ISBN 978-1-4271-9396-4 (pdf).--ISBN 978-1-4271-9390-2 (html)

    1. Fetal alcohol syndrome--Juvenile literature.
I. Gowsell, Rosie, 1975- , author II. Title.

RG629.F45R64 2014   j618.3'26861   C2013-907587-9
                                                 C2013-907588-7

Library of Congress Cataloging-in-Publication Data

Rodger, Ellen, author.
 Fetal alcohol spectrum disorder / Ellen Rodger and Rosie
Gowsell.
      pages cm. -- (Understanding mental health)
 Audience: Age 10-13.
 Audience: Grades 7 to 8.
 Includes index.
 ISBN 978-0-7787-0083-8 (reinforced library binding) -- ISBN
978-0-7787-0089-0 (pbk.) -- ISBN 978-1-4271-9396-4 (electronic
pdf) -- ISBN 978-1-4271-9390-2 (electronic html)
 1. Fetal alcohol syndrome--Juvenile literature. I. Gowsell,
Rosie. II. Title.

RG629.F45R63 2014
618.3'26861--dc23
                                                 2013043398

Crabtree Publishing Company

www.crabtreebooks.com   1-800-387-7650

Printed in Canada/012014/BF20131120

Published in Canada
Crabtree Publishing
616 Welland Ave.
St. Catharines, ON
L2M 5V6

Published in the United States
Crabtree Publishing
PMB 59051
350 Fifth Avenue, 59th Floor
New York, New York 10118

Published in the United Kingdom
Crabtree Publishing
Maritime House
Basin Road North, Hove
BN41 1WR

Published in Australia
Crabtree Publishing
3 Charles Street
Coburg North
VIC, 3058

CONTENTS

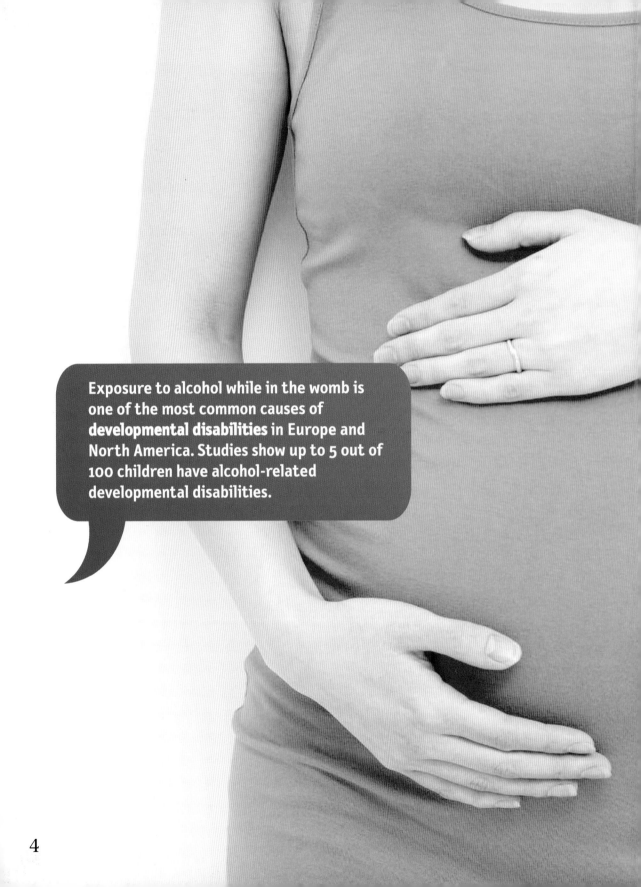

Exposure to alcohol while in the womb is one of the most common causes of **developmental disabilities** in Europe and North America. Studies show up to 5 out of 100 children have alcohol-related developmental disabilities.

In My Brain

"I know I'm different. I'm different because I have FASD. My foster parents found out I had it when I was six. My birth mom had a problem with alcohol and drank when she was pregnant with me. The alcohol damaged my brain. It's permanent and I won't grow out of it. When I was younger I had a hard time in school. It's hard for me to learn math and I can't remember some things. Actually, I can't remember a lot. But I can learn and I am really good at some things.

It's hard for me to make friends because I don't always understand people and they don't understand me. I get frustrated with things sometimes and it makes me freak out. This frightens people. I don't mean to do it and I don't want to do it. But it happens and I feel bad about myself after."

—Richard, age 14.

A Disability Nobody Wants to Talk About

When people think of developmental disabilities, they usually think about **Autism Spectrum Disorder** or **Attention Deficit Hyperactivity Disorder** (ADHD). These are disorders that get a lot of media coverage. Fetal Alcohol Spectrum Disorder (FASD) is the leading cause of developmental disabilities, yet many people don't want to think or talk about the disorder. That's because the **stigma** with FASD is enormous. FASD is preventable. It is caused by drinking alcohol while pregnant and can lead to feelings of shame, anger, and fear. Mothers who drank during pregnancy and caused harm to their unborn children feel shame. The children who must live with the symptoms of FASD may also feel shame, but fear and anger are other common emotions.

A Spectrum

FASD is a spectrum disorder, which means there are a wide array of effects and impacts on each individual. One person with the disorder may have difficulty controlling their **impulses**, while another may be born severely brain damaged or blind.

The brain is a complex organ. No two people with FASD are the same, due to the variations in how alcohol affects the developing brain.

Different but Good

People with FASD are not "bad seeds." They are also not stupid. Their brains work differently, which can make life more difficult for them. Imagine not being able to remember something you were just told, or not understanding the concept of time. You would have to work ten times harder just to answer questions in class or arrive at school on time. That is the reality for someone with FASD—they must work harder than everyone else to adjust to the world around them.

Sometimes kids just want to be like everybody else. It's difficult to blend in when you have a disability that affects the way you perceive the world and how you act.

FASD is a term for many conditions. All the conditions are grouped under one name or "umbrella."

8

What Is FASD?

chapter 1

Doctors and **psychologists** describe FASD as "a range of permanent birth defects and brain damage caused by maternal alcohol consumption." In other words, FASD is a group of conditions that occur in individuals whose mothers drank alcohol during pregnancy. These conditions include Fetal Alcohol Syndrome, Partial Fetal Alcohol Syndrome, Alcohol-Related Neurodevelopmental Disorder, and Alcohol-Related Birth Defects. Some people who have FASD have birth defects such as blindness. Others have problems controlling their behavior or learning new things. Most often, people with FASD have a mix of physical and learning difficulties.

The Complex Brain

The brain of a person with FASD has been permanently damaged. It cannot be "cured" at this point in time. That's a scary fact. But the encouraging news is that brain research is constantly expanding. Scientists are learning more every day about how the brain works. With ongoing research, there is hope that in the future we can help the brain to repair itself. One thing we know right now is that everybody's brain functions differently. That's why no two people with FASD are exactly alike.

"I'm not stupid, but it takes me longer to learn things. One thing I have had to learn is that I need help and that, if I accept help, I can do things. One of the things I like to do and I am good at is photography. I had an educational assistant who taught me photography. She taught me that photography is only part remembering steps and, if one day I can't remember things like aperture, I can still play around and take pictures and see things from my eyes. I have a good eye for pictures."

— Vaughn, 16.

Can't, Not Won't

The brains of people with FASD work differently, so these people therefore behave differently. It may be hard for people with FASD to sit down quietly and learn in a classroom. They may seem too friendly or get overly aggressive and **dismissive** of rules. It is important to realize that these are not things they have control over and they are not just being difficult. People with **cerebral palsy** cannot control they way their bodies move and we must think of FASD in a similar way. It's not that people with FASD won't listen or do something, it's that they can't do it.

The Effects of FASD

FASD has primary, secondary, and tertiary (or third) characteristics, or effects.

Primary Characteristics/Effects: In the case of FASD, primary characteristics are the things that are caused by a brain damaged from alcohol. They include difficulties with language and learning, attention, memory, **reasoning**, and understanding. Primary effects are often mistaken as behavior problems, but they are a brain damage disability. Some examples or results of primary characteristics or effects include:

Learning disabilities—not being able to learn, keep, or remember things like other people.

Difficulty controlling impulses—such as blurting out things in class or grabbing things that don't belong to them.

Poor or inconsistent memory—such as not being able to remember something you just learned.

Being oversensitive to some things and undersensitive to others—some people with FASD can't stand the feeling of their own clothing on their skin, while others aren't aware of physical pain when they hurt themselves.

Physical disabilities—some people with FASD have vision or hearing problems, smaller heads, and kidney or liver problems.

Hyperactivity and Dysmaturity—some people with FASD are easily distracted, or have difficulty with problem solving. They may also show signs of dysmaturity, or being developmentally younger than their age.

Secondary Characteristics

Secondary characteristics are effects or disabilities that arise later for people with FASD. They are a reaction to "not fitting into" society. Most are not part of the brain damage of FASD. They are sometimes defensive behaviors that are the result of **inadequate** coping abilities. Imagine knowing there is something different about the way you learn—that you can't retain information, or understand something no matter how hard you try. Then imagine if nobody knows how to help you. You'd soon start to feel you are a miserable failure. Sometimes people will actually tell you that you won't amount to much. That's how many people with FASD feel, particularly if they have never been diagnosed and given adequate supports for learning and living.

The saying "if you judge a fish on its ability to climb a tree, it will live its whole life believing that it is stupid" is a good way of thinking about how people with FASD learn.

Protection from Pain

Secondary characteristics include acting out, anxiety, frustration, shutting down, and using drugs and alcohol to cope. Other secondary characteristics include destructive behaviors such as throwing or breaking things, being fearful, or avoiding things that cause pain or fear. Many of these characteristics can be prevented or lessened with the right support. They are protective or defensive actions for people with FASD—they are merely protecting themselves from emotional pain. This means that a person with FASD who has an early diagnosis, a supportive family, and schools that work with their disability and not against it, can learn to manage a lot of pain and suffering.

Frustration, Acting Out, and Tantrums

Knowing you are different and that you can't do what other people ask you to do can make you upset and annoyed. This frustration can boil over into uncontrollable fits and tantrums as the FASD brain struggles to sort the feelings and cope.

Disrupted School Experience

School isn't an easy place for kids with FASD. A lot of learning is based on memory and the ability to understand **abstract** ideas, or ideas that have to be visualized or imagined in your head. When you just can't do the exact things a teacher or a school asks you to do, you learn pretty quickly that school isn't the place for you.

People with FASD, particularly those who were never diagnosed, have a hard time adapting to the rules and formats of school. Since time is an abstract concept, they may not understand how to budget their time. Fifteen minutes may feel like a nanosecond, or an eternity. They may be late for school because they can't get organized and ready, no matter how hard they try. They may miss school and learning and, as a result, drop out early. The thing is, if a school can adapt to the learning styles of a child with FASD, a child with FASD can learn and be successful. This success can carry on into the adolescent and teen years.

Kids with FASD may disrupt the class. They might also be distant, sad, or fearful. Sometimes, they are all of these things in one day.

14

When the Frustration Doesn't End

Think about what it might feel like to know you are different, but to also have no idea why. You might not be able to understand things like everybody else, or you can't finish your work because you keep forgetting the instructions. Now imagine feeling like this every day, all of the time. It's pretty easy to see how someone would get frustrated with themselves and give up. The long-term effects of FASD are called tertiary characteristics. They are the result of ongoing frustration and failure—particularly when the person with FASD has not been diagnosed and has never had support to cope with their brain damage. It can be horrible to go through life with people thinking you deliberately do bad things and that you could stop doing them if you only tried. But that is what happens when people view FASD as a behavior that people can change instead of a physical disability like being deaf or blind.

Like secondary characteristics, tertiary characteristics can be prevented or made less severe. They include such things as mental health disorders, incarceration (time in prison), running away from home, problems with employment and living independently, inappropriate sexual behavior, and unplanned teen pregnancy.

Mental Health Disorders

The stress and fear caused by not understanding or fitting into the world can contribute to conditions such as anxiety and depression. There is evidence that suggests that the exposure to alcohol while in the womb increases the likelihood of depressive disorders for children and adults with FASD. Studies also show that children with FASD have higher rates of ADHD and **Oppositional Defiant Disorder** (ODD). The presence of two or more illnesses or disabilities at the same time is called comorbidity.

Substance Abuse and Addictions

Some teens like to experiment with alcohol and drugs. The FASD brain was damaged by exposure to alcohol and many people with FASD may be more **susceptible** to substance addictions because of this exposure. Some turn to alcohol or drugs to ease the emotional pain of not fitting in, but quickly develop an addiction to the exact drug that gave them brain damage before they were born.

Trouble with the Law

An estimated 55 percent of the people in prison today have FASD. That's a frightening statistic. FASD doesn't make people bad. It doesn't give them a "criminal mind." In fact, people with FASD are likely to be more trusting and less **devious** than people who do not have FASD. FASD affects reasoning and judgment. A person with FASD is more vulnerable to the **manipulation** and the persuasion of others.

Being Vulnerable

If teens with FASD are out with friends, they could be easily convinced to steal a few dollars from someone because they don't understand the meaning and value of money. FASD prevents them from understanding abstract concepts such as "cause and effect" and "crime and punishment." They could easily commit a crime and not understand what would happen if they got caught. They might have been told the consequences, but they can't understand or they forget.

Sexual Inappropriateness

The adolescent and teen years are a time of great change for everybody. Bodies and minds are developing emotionally, physically, and hormonally. The hormone surges that occur before and during puberty can be difficult to deal with for someone with FASD. Their emotional or social development has not kept pace with their physical development. In other words, they may have the body of a teenager but the emotions and social understanding of a child. Their poor impulse control means they may make unwanted sexual advances without understanding it is wrong to do so. They may touch inappropriately, or allow inappropriate touching by others. This doesn't mean that if you have FASD you will automatically act inappropriately. But learning to control your impulses is a major part of dealing with FASD.

This same lack of control over impulses means teens with FASD may also be more at risk for an unplanned pregnancy.

Building trusting relationships is important to youth with FASD.

Independent Living

Some children and adults with FASD have such severe brain damage that they need full-time caregivers to look after their basic needs. Others need more gentle supports, such as help budgeting, planning, and organizing their lives. As a spectrum disorder, each person's brain damage and **deficits** are different.

The disorder can make it hard for some people to get and keep jobs. Most jobs usually require that workers always arrive on time, remember what they are supposed to do, and work well without direction. These are the exact things an FASD brain just cannot do on its own. The truth is, many people with FASD need supports for their entire life to help them meet their potential. Living independently may be a challenge for some, but not one that can't be managed. You can finish school, go to college, and hold a job if you have FASD—but you will need help and an environment that accepts your FASD as a physical disability and not something that you can just fix through hard work.

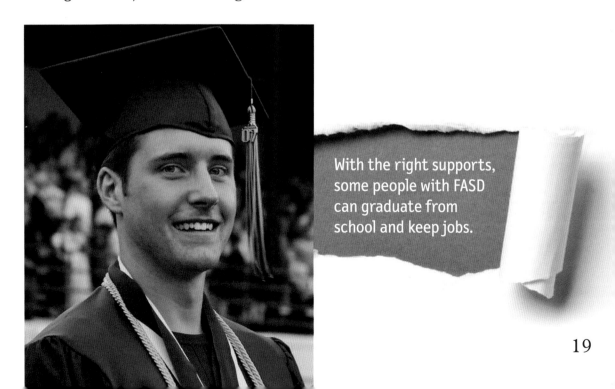

With the right supports, some people with FASD can graduate from school and keep jobs.

Fetal Alcohol Spectrum Disorder is a group of conditions related by one common cause: alcohol use by pregnant women.

Chapter 2

Diagnosis and Treatment

FASD is the world's leading cause of preventable birth defects. An estimated one percent of all babies born in the United States each year have Fetal Alcohol Syndrome (FAS). One in 100 babies born in Canada has FASD.

Despite all we know about this disability, diagnosing it is still difficult. The reason for this lies partly in the fact that up to 80 percent of people with FASD are not raised by their birth parents. Doctors may not know whether the birth mother drank alcohol when pregnant. In many areas of the world, inducing the U.S., only Fetal Alcohol Syndrome—one disorder in the FASD spectrum—has specific guidelines that doctors follow for diagnosis. Some patients may have a FASD, but do not "fit" the diagnosis guidelines for FAS.

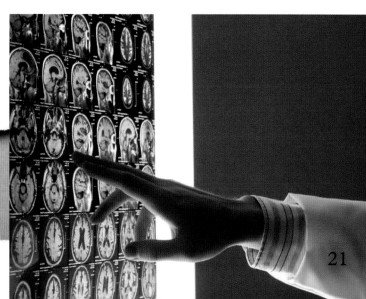

FASD requires both medical and behavioral help from doctors and psychologists.

Getting Diagnosed

So why is a diagnosis important? Early diagnosis can change how a person with FASD lives and learns. Studies show being diagnosed as a child greatly improves the outcomes for someone with FASD. With a diagnosis comes targeting treatment plans that can help a person with FASD learn more effectively, cope better, and possibly avoid the secondary and tertiary effects of the disability. Diagnosis gives those with FASD a fighting chance.

"Diagnosis was scary but it was also freeing because then we knew what we were up against and we could join with other parents and find support. When you know things and have a plan, you can deal. You can fight for a future."

— Sheila, parent.

Under the Umbrella

FASD is an umbrella term for five different disorders: Fetal Alcohol Syndrome (FAS), Partial FAS (pFAS), Alcohol-Related Neurodevelopmental Disorder (ARND), Fetal Alcohol Effects (FAE), and Alcohol-Related Birth Defects (ARBD). All of the disorders have one common cause, but the specific brain damage results in different disabilities. For FAS, doctors look for physical signs such as small head in relation to body size, skin folds at the corner of the eye, thin upper lip, or smoothness or no groove between the nose and upper lip. They also take into account a patient's developmental deficits, or mental or physical disabilities, and whether there are problems with social skills or paying attention. It is important to note that you can have FASD and not look any different than anyone else. And FASD can be overlooked or misdiagnosed.

Team Effort

FASD is diagnosed by a doctor or a child psychiatrist—a doctor who has special training in childhood mental illness and brain disorders. Sometimes, a team of mental health professionals will help doctors make a diagnosis. The team might include specialist doctors, psychologists, or social workers, as well as therapists and speech and language specialists who have knowledge and understanding of the disability. This team will gather information about a patient and help conduct tests, or assessments to diagnose the specific disorder in the spectrum. They can also determine the severity of the disability.

An FASD assessment usually has several steps including a medical examination, and tests to determine the type and degree of brain damage. Once an assessment and diagnosis are made, the doctor or team can develop a plan of action for the person with FASD.

What Happens Next?

FASD is a lifelong condition that requires lifelong treatment. Diagnosis is an essential part of getting support and learning how to manage behavior. Once people with FASD learn to cope with their disability, they have better chances of reaching their potential. Supports are key and they include ongoing assessments by doctors, psychologists, and therapists. Not everyone with FASD has the same disabilities or challenges. One person may have problems with cognition, or how they understand or "see" things. Another may have a hearing problem, a heart problem, and difficulties focusing on tasks. This means there is no cookie-cutter approach to providing supports.

FASD and Other Disorders

Often, a person with FASD will be dealing with other disorders at the same time. This is called a co-occurring disorder. One example is FASD and ADHD, a brain-based disorder that makes it difficult for a person to sit still, focus, and think clearly. Doctors will treat the symptoms of each disorder with prescription drugs and the most useful therapies.

Stigma is serious. The fear and shame of a diagnosis can prevent people from seeking treatment— which only makes things worse.

Chapter 3

Dealing With Stigma

There shouldn't be any shame associated with FASD or any other medical disorder or disability, but there is. People with FASD are sometimes ridiculed and made to feel that they are stupid or **incompetent**, and that they will never amount to much. Stigma is the shame or judgmental attitudes associated with a certain disease, disorder, or condition. The stigma that FASD carries is doubly dangerous as it can lead to self-hate. People with FASD might begin to believe that the negative comments from others are true. They may begin to treat themselves badly because others treat them badly. The pain of not fitting into society can lead to tertiary characteristics in people with FASD. When you try hard and still fail, you begin to think the snarky things people think and say are correct. It is a vicious circle.

Stigma Hurts

Stigma hurts everyone. It hurts the person with FASD, as well as their parents, siblings, and friends. One of the causes of stigma is fear. People fear what they don't know or understand. This fear leads to rejection and exclusion. A kid with FASD may be excluded from a group because people fear his or her behavior may be difficult to deal with, or that it will make them feel awkward or uncomfortable. But FASD is largely invisible. People who have it are judged because others view their actions simply as behaviors that they could have control over if they tried, and not as a disability caused by brain damage.

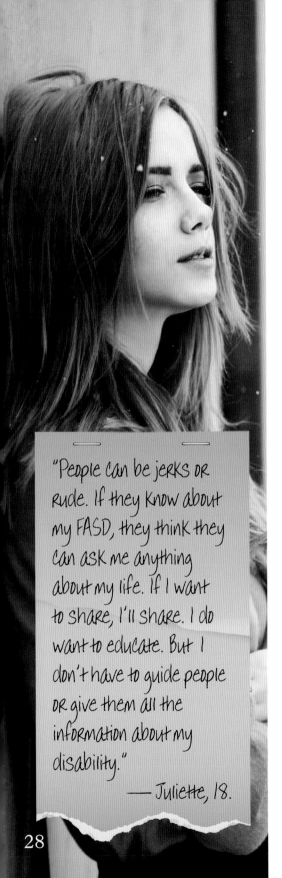

"People can be jerks or rude. If they know about my FASD, they think they can ask me anything about my life. If I want to share, I'll share. I do want to educate. But I don't have to guide people or give them all the information about my disability."

— Juliette, 18.

Combatting Stigma

One way to combat the stigma of FASD is to be open about it. Although it shouldn't be the job of the person with FASD (or their family) to educate people about the disorder, sometimes people just don't know what it is. Sometimes families and the person with FASD are the only people who have the knowledge to educate others. If you have FASD and someone asks you "what's wrong with you?" you can answer them simply, with, "I have a disability called FASD. You can look it up and read about it."

Hey Buddy!

Friendships are important to all of us and that's no different for people who have FASD. People with FASD want to fit in. They want to be themselves and be understood and accepted. This means accepting their differences. It's difficult for someone with FASD to think the way other people do. They get frustrated by things that others take for granted. How much better would it be if people with FASD felt that they belonged and that they mattered?

An Ounce of Prevention...

FASD has no cure, but it can be prevented. It has one cause: drinking alcohol while pregnant. That fact adds to the stigma of the disorder—that someone caused it and is therefore responsible for the outcome. But as FASD advocate Morgan Fawcett has said: "there are no perpetrators with FASD, only victims." The victims include children born with FASD, their families, caregivers, and their mothers—many of whom feel terrible guilt because they drank alcohol while pregnant. FASD advocates such as Morgan help to remove the stigma of the disability and educate people about its cause. The goal is to prevent FASD, but just telling people not to drink while they are pregnant isn't enough. Some women may be addicted to alcohol and are more likely to have unprotected sex that could lead to pregnancy. They need help to end their addiction. Others may even have been told by their doctors that a little bit of alcohol once in awhile is okay. But the truth is, no amount of alcohol is safe to drink while pregnant. It may only take an ounce of alcohol to permanently damage a baby's developing brain.

Information campaigns make the point that it doesn't matter if a pregnant woman is a binge drinker or only has an occasional drink, the result is the same: drinking while pregnant can have a lifetime of consequences. This is why it is doubly important not to engage in unprotected sex and drinking. You might not know you are pregnant when you are drinking, so it is best not to take the risk.

Following a schedule that is written down and posted on a wall can help a person with FASD stay focused and organized.

Chapter 4

Managing Behavior

So, you're in class and the sights, smells, and sounds of 25 people scraping chairs, tapping pens, or whispering is driving you crazy. There's too many things going on and you can't concentrate. What do you do? You develop some supports and strategies to help you focus. People with FASD can be easily overwhelmed by ordinary situations that may not bother other people. This can result in unpredictable behavior. Supports and strategies are key to being focused and calm.

Strategy 1: Develop Routines

Routines are organized patterns for doing things. They can help you get things done, but they are also useful because they keep your brain from overloading. The FASD brain has difficulty absorbing information, processing or interpreting information, and making decisions based on that information. A routine helps you understand by giving you a pattern to follow for each day and each activity. People who don't have FASD follow routines too, but they might not even realize it. When you break each part of the day down into tasks, it is a lot easier to manage, and you know what to expect.

Schedule

SUN	MON	TUE	WED	THU	FRI	SAT

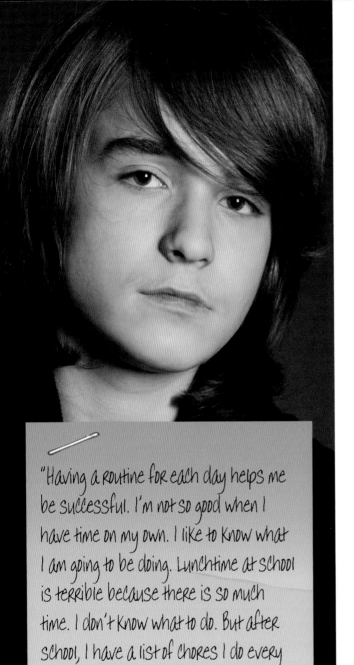

"Having a routine for each day helps me be successful. I'm not so good when I have time on my own. I like to know what I am going to be doing. Lunchtime at school is terrible because there is so much time. I don't know what to do. But after school, I have a list of chores I do every day. I feed my dog and walk him. After, I play a video game then do homework, then eat supper. After supper I get ready for bed."

— Rayne, 16.

Strategy 2: Calming

When there is just too much going on in a classroom or other setting—it's too busy with people, or too noisy—a person with FASD may find it difficult to control their frustration. Developing their own calming strategy allows people with FASD to recognize their feelings and prevent outbursts. A calming strategy may involve having a place in a classroom (back of the room for example) where they can go and sit with headphones on. Other calming solutions include:

- Keeping a comfy item of clothing such as a hoodie, on hand that they can wrap around themselves.

- "Spotters" or classroom friends who can watch for signs of frustration and alert the teacher.

- Dark sunglasses for cutting down outside visual "noise" and limiting stimulation.

Keeping Calm and Focused

ROUTINE CONSISTENCY: Keep daily and even hourly routines. Routines will help you keep calm because you will know what to expect.

DRAW IT OUT: It may be difficult to remember the steps in a routine, so you may need visual hints such as line drawings of a task. A line drawing of a shower will help you remember to shower in the morning after you wake up. A line drawing of a clothes hamper may help you remember where to put your dirty laundry at home.

EXERCISE: Many people with FASD are fidgety and find it stressful to learn or take in information when they are sitting down. Physical activity is important in relieving stress. Exercise releases **endorphins** that make dealing with frustration easier—but it should be exercise they enjoy.

KNOWING YOUR EMOTIONS: It may be hard for a person with FASD to identify feelings (their own and other people's). For example, they may not connect the tenseness they feel in their muscles to feeling angry. Making a dictionary that uses images to visually illustrate emotions can help a person with FASD connect and identify emotions.

SLEEP: Sleep helps your body restore and heal itself, and helps your brain work. Sleeping can be difficult for people with FASD. Maintaining a regular sleep routine can help. This includes getting ready for bed and going to sleep at around the same time every night.

It's better to have one or two true friends than a bunch of people you hang out with but who don't really know or care about you.

Chapter 5
Making Friends

WANTED: Trusting friend with a devil-may-care attitude who likes to have fun and please people. Sound like a plea for the perfect pal? It could also be a description of an adolescent or teen friend with FASD. Many people with FASD are overly trusting, easily manipulated, and eager to impress.

The teen years can be difficult, and even more so if you have FASD. Making and keeping friends can be a challenge for people with FASD because it is more difficult for them to "read" people, or understand common social situations. Adolescents and teens with FASD are less emotionally mature than other youths the same age. This makes it hard for them to relate. They will often trust people they shouldn't trust, and do things to impress or make people happy. A teenage girl with FASD might for example, interpret a friendly wave and a smile from a boy as "he's my boyfriend." A teen boy might be more likely to do dangerous stunts such as jumping off high things, or doing crazy tricks, to impress friends.

Trying to Fit In

Adolescents and teens with FASD may also act impulsively in social situations—grabbing a person, speaking too loudly, acting too friendly, or interrupting others. This can be interpreted as rudeness—even though they're not meaning to be rude. It's a part of the disability, and it's something that people are not aware of. Not that young people with a disability always want others to know about it. Often, teens with FASD would prefer people didn't know because they fear being judged as simple. That's why they will go to lengths to try to "act" like their friends. It's fantastic when the friends are mature, caring, and supportive, but not so great when the friends take advantage of their innocent and trusting nature.

Friends 101

Wouldn't it be great if there were friendship rules that everyone had to follow? Knowing how to make friends is difficult for people with FASD. Here are some tips for trusting:

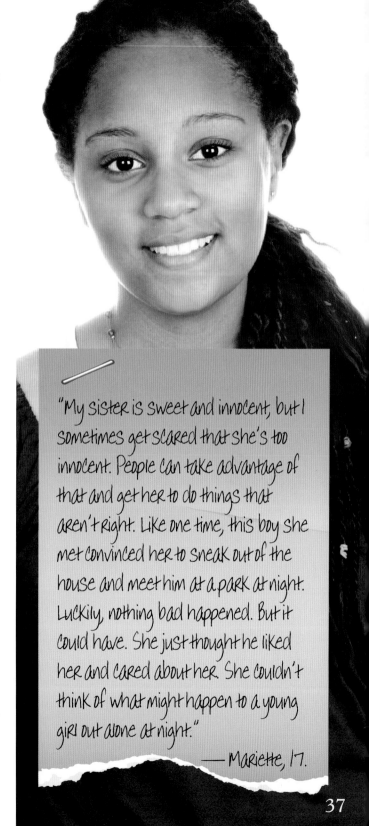

- Learn to recognize body language and expressions by looking at books and magazines. Work to understand how people say things without words. Ask someone you trust to help you by play acting different emotions.

- Be honest about your disability. If people can't accept who you are, they won't be good friends.

- Believe that you can be a good friend too.

- Join clubs that have trusted adult supervisors so that you can learn how to join and be a part of a group. Be sure the adult understands FASD.

"My sister is sweet and innocent, but I sometimes get scared that she's too innocent. People can take advantage of that and get her to do things that aren't right. Like one time, this boy she met convinced her to sneak out of the house and meet him at a park at night. Luckily, nothing bad happened. But it could have. She just thought he liked her and cared about her. She couldn't think of what might happen to a young girl out alone at night."

— Mariette, 17.

A support system, with an "external brain" or someone who helps "think" is vital for people with FASD.

Chapter 6

Family Ties

For a person with FASD, family—birth family, foster family, or adopted family—is their support system. Family members help them translate the world and function appropriately within it. Friends, therapists, teachers, and educational assistants who understand how someone with FASD acts and learns are also a part of the support system. Living with or being a friend to someone with FASD can at times be difficult and exhausting. A loved one with FASD may need you to help them communicate, keep on schedule, and sometimes tell them basic things such as when and how to eat. FASD is a disability that affects all aspects of life—not just for the person who has it, but for those who love and care for them.

Reframing Things

One of the first things a loved one has to learn about FASD is that the behaviors that accompany the disability are not about choice. FASD isn't a *won't do* situation, it's a *can't do* situation. You can't change the damage done to their brain, but you can help change the situation or the environment they live in. This means reframing things. If your child or sibling with FASD freaks out at surprise parties, don't have surprise parties. Changes in routine can throw them. If the party is meant as a surprise for someone else, let them in on the plan and prepare them for what is going to happen. There's no guarantee things will go smoothly, but at least there will be a plan.

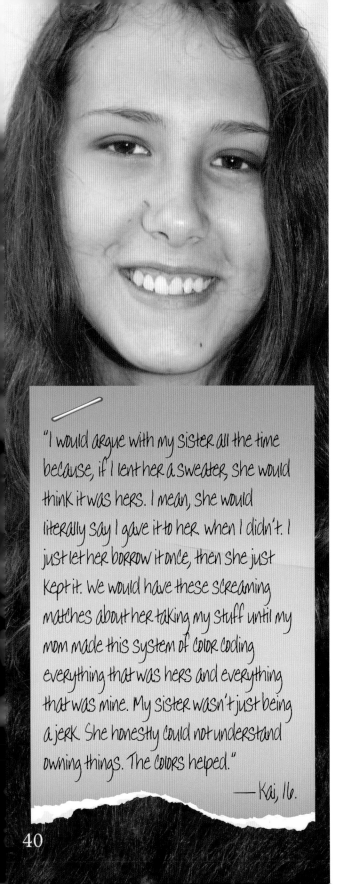

"I would argue with my sister all the time because, if I lent her a sweater, she would think it was hers. I mean, she would literally say I gave it to her when I didn't. I just let her borrow it once, then she just kept it. We would have these screaming matches about her taking my stuff until my mom made this system of color coding everything that was hers and everything that was mine. My sister wasn't just being a jerk. She honestly could not understand owning things. The colors helped."

—Kai, 16.

Getting Frustrated

Hey, nobody's a saint. It's not easy trying to make life more equal for someone with FASD. It's normal to feel frustrated, angry, and ripped off when everything seems to be about your sibling with FASD.

If your parents are busy dealing with your brother or sister's needs, it may seem like your needs don't matter. Or maybe you are tired of arguing with your brother or sister. It's okay to ask for time and space away from them. In fact, it is helpful to have someone you trust such as a teacher, counselor, friend, grandparent, or other close relative to talk to about your frustrations. It's important that you have someone in your corner.

Just remember that you are important. Your sibling needs to feel loved by those they trust. It's important that they know they have someone on their side too.

On Equality

Having a disability does not mean a person is incapable. It means they need more supports to be equal. Equality is not simple acceptance. Equality requires changing the environment so that the person with the disability can live their life like people who do not have a disability. For example, if you were blind, you would not be able to read books made for people who could see. You would learn to read by using a system called braille, that was designed for blind people. People with FASD learn and act differently too. In order for them to be equal, we need to change the way we interact with them, determine a system that works, and stick with it.

Do What Works for You

Some people with FASD call their caregivers who support them their "external brains." It's a funny way of saying that caregivers have to think for them and help them navigate life. Here are some things you can do to care for your loved one and yourself:

- Have "me time" as a part of your daily or weekly routine. Me time can mean going to a movie alone or with a friend, or just scheduling an hour to read a book.

- Let extended family members know that equality for your FASD child means adhering to their schedules or routines for events and gatherings. If they can't do that for a few hours, then they aren't interested in accepting your child.

- Don't beat yourself up if your child or sibling has a meltdown with you. You may be the only person they feel safe enough with to do so.

41

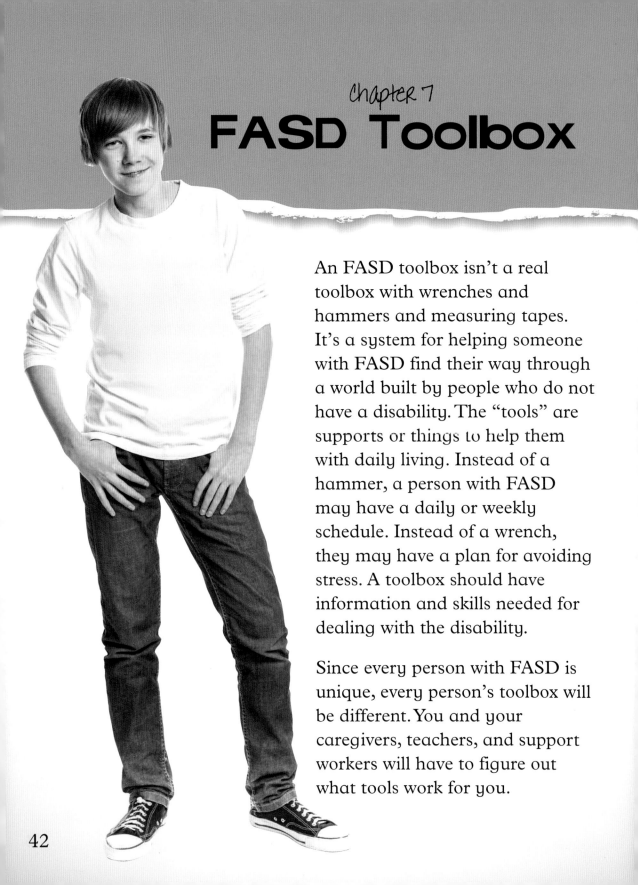

Chapter 7

FASD Toolbox

An FASD toolbox isn't a real toolbox with wrenches and hammers and measuring tapes. It's a system for helping someone with FASD find their way through a world built by people who do not have a disability. The "tools" are supports or things to help them with daily living. Instead of a hammer, a person with FASD may have a daily or weekly schedule. Instead of a wrench, they may have a plan for avoiding stress. A toolbox should have information and skills needed for dealing with the disability.

Since every person with FASD is unique, every person's toolbox will be different. You and your caregivers, teachers, and support workers will have to figure out what tools work for you.

Pack Your Toolbox

A toolbox can include anything that helps you function. With FASD, it is often useful to have visual organizers and cues that can help remind you of things you have to do and also give instructions on how to do them.

UNDERSTANDING TIME:
Time is difficult to understand if you need to see and touch things to learn. You can learn time by association. Your morning routine may take an hour. Ask your caregiver to break the hour down on a face of a clock. You get up at 7 a.m. and wash up until 7:15 a.m. That's fifteen minutes. Follow the same routine each morning and break the hour down on the clock until you know it. Or use an egg timer to time activities. When the timer goes off, it is time to move on to the next activity.

ANTI-FIDGET STRATEGY:
Often, people with FASD find it difficult to keep still and concentrate. Some find that squeezing a stress ball, or bean bag can calm them and stop the fidgeting. Earplugs or headphones can also work to block out sounds when working.

BE PREPARED:
Plan for the day and have your caregiver or teacher let you know a few minutes beforehand that a class or task will be ending. This will give you time to transition to the next task.

USE A CALENDAR:
Use a weekly calendar that splits the day into morning, afternoon, and evening. This will help you understand when activities will happen.

GET SOCIAL:
Rehearse or act out socially acceptable behavior until it becomes normal.

Decisions, Decisions

Making decisions comes easy to people who do not have FASD, but youth with FASD need a longer time to learn and make good decisions. It's best to think things over. You may really want that candy bar, but you don't have money to buy it and pay for your bus fare too. What do you do? Do you want to walk home? If not, use the money for bus fare. If you make a mistake and buy the candy bar, you will have to walk home.

Change of Plans

Your friend is supposed to meet you at the library after school. When they aren't at the library door, you don't know what to do so you just stand there and can't move. Unexpected changes of plan or routine are a part of life. Planning for problems can help ease stress and so can communicating your needs with others. Your friends should be told that they need to follow through on plans with you. If they can't, they should let an adult know so that they can tell you.

Planning ahead for emergencies or problems will help a person with FASD manage their behavior.

Memory Minders

You can't always trust your memory if you have FASD. You may have trouble remembering when assignments are due or what time you are supposed to meet someone. Writing things down in an appointment book, calendar, or agenda can jog your memory. Make it a habit to look through your appointment book every day in the morning and afternoon. Use pictures and visuals to remind you of the event. For example, a birthday cake sticker can be a reminder that it is someone's birthday.

Money Matters

Parents usually complain that all teens are "bad" with managing money. But people with FASD have more trouble than most. Understanding the value of money is difficult, so you will need to use tools such as a calculator and a notebook to keep track of spending. Go grocery shopping with your parent or caregiver and write down in your notebook the price of everything that is put into the cart. Add the totals up. This will help you understand that everything in the cart costs money.

Other Resources

It can be hard to find reliable information on FASD. Check your library for books. Make sure they are books that were recently published. Old books won't have the latest research and information. Ask your parent or caregiver to help you check the Internet for websites and hotlines that are geared to your age group. Be careful when searching websites. Not every site gives factual information. Here are some good resources to start with:

Helpful Hotlines
National Organization on Fetal Alcohol Syndrome
1-800-666-6327

This is a toll free (U.S.) hotline that provides information and referrals for people with questions about FASD. The NOFAS website at www.nofas.org has a resource directory of state organizations that provide information on diagnosis and FASD advocacy.

National Suicide Hotline
1-800-SUICIDE (784-2433)

This toll-free 24-hour national service connects you to a trained counselor at a nearby suicide crisis center. The service is confidential. Also try the Adolescent Suicide Hotline: 800-621-4000.

Kids Help Phone
1-800-668-6868

A free, confidential, 24-hour hotline staffed by professional counselors. Supports youths who are in crisis and need help and information on a number of issues. Hotline available in Canada only. Visit their website at www.kidshelpphone.ca.

Websites
Centers for Disease Control and Prevention
www.cdc.gov/ncbddd/kids/index.html

The Kids' Quest section provides information, quick facts, and directions to other sites, movies, and books that have information on FASD.

Kids Health Organization
www.kidshealth.org/parent/medical/brain/fas.html
#cat20073

A site with information in English and Spanish on fetal alcohol syndrome and alcohol as a drug and its effects on the brain and overall health.

Mind Your Mind
mindyourmind.ca

An informational teen-oriented mental health and related disorders site with information on getting help and personal stories about coping, struggles and successes, a blog, and interactive tools that can help you identify and cope with your symptoms.

Glossary

abstract Something, such as time, that exists as an idea but does not have a concrete or physical form

Attention Deficit Hyperactivity Disorder A behavioral disorder with symptoms that include difficulty staying focused and paying attention

Autism Spectrum Disorder A group of developmental brain disorders in which someone may have difficulty communicating and understanding abstract concepts

cerebral palsy A disorder that affects movement and muscle tone that is usually caused by brain damage at or before birth

deficits Mental or physical impairments

developmental disabilities Physical, mental, or neurological disabilities that appear before a person reaches age 22

devious Dishonest or underhanded

dismissive Actions or beliefs that show something is not important or worth an effort

endorphins Substances in the brain that can activate during exercise and make a person feel happy

impulses Sudden and strong urges to do something

inadequate Not enough of something

incompetent Not having the skills to do something well

manipulation Control or unfair influence over something or someone

Oppositional Defiant Disorder A disorder in childhood where a person is angry and hostile, particularly to people in authority such as parents or teachers

psychologists An expert in the study of human behavior

reasoning The action of thinking about something

stigma Shame associated with a particular disorder or behavior

susceptible Easily influenced by someone or something

Index